Library of Congress Cataloging-in-Publication Data: Available.
ISBN-13: 978-1-948830-38-6 / ISBN-10: 1-948830-38-8

This project is supported in part by an award from the National Endowment for the Arts and the New York State Council on the Arts with the support of Governor Andrew M. Cuomo and the New York State Legislature.

The translation and publication of this book was made possible through funding from the Daesan Foundation.

Printed on acid-free paper in the United States of America.

Cover Design by Jenny Volvovski
Interior Design by Anthony Blake

Open Letter is the University of Rochester's nonprofit, literary translation press:
Dewey Hall 1-219, Box 278968, Rochester, NY 14627

www.openletterbooks.org

CATCALLING

LEE SOHO

Translated from the Korean by Soje

OPEN LETTER
LITERARY TRANSLATIONS FROM THE UNIVERSITY OF ROCHESTER

Surely they'll go to hell
for making us sad.

TABLE OF CONTENTS

PART 1
KYUNGJIN'S HOME

COHABITATION

I was born but somehow you were born too. From one to two. We crumple ourselves into the cramped stroller.

We use the same uniform, man, room.

Unni, the doctor says I should do whatever I want. So Unni, I'm not going to call you Unni anymore. Because I love you, I'm going to call you by your name. Let's be real, you don't deserve to be called a big sister, my little sister says, peeling the apple with a knife. It's the last apple, so you better finish it. Little sister points the knife at me as she peels the apple. Crunchcrunch I eat the apple.

I slit little sister's wrist for her. Mom says you slept inside her like it was your grave. I slit little sister's wrist again. Hush little baby. You're prettiest when you sleep. I put her to sleep on her stomach. I put her to sleep, pulling the blanket to the top of her head. How cramped how cramped the night is. From one to two. From one to two.

DAY WITHOUT REDUCTION

At night I thought of day
I thought of the moth dead inside the fluorescent lamp
A faint and faraway life
Before the innumerable 0 we

count the corpses of the monkfish lying diagonally,
discarded on our dining table
I carve out the eye of the souring monkfish We make a
broth with all the right and wrong doings of the monkfish
and drink it up for dinner We spread them wide open and dig
around and
close them I

debone the moldy monkfish and eat its tender flesh In the
kitchen Mom removes the skin and dresses me in it I become
a bag and a bank account
and a husband too Mom holds my hand only after putting
on rubber gloves on top of cotton gloves
Finish your food You should eat the bones too Mom
opens my mouth and feeds me her teat to wash it all down I
spill a mouthful of milk and wear my milk-splashed panties
and shove my milk-splashed finger down my throat What
floatfloats unswallowed is my
tongue

Mom weeps like a roll of toilet paper

I thought about Mom
and the spoonfuls of monkfish
I thought about the day without any
reduction

Without fail
at night I thought of day
At the table we recalled
growing kinder in unfamiliar places

FEARING THE GAZE OF STRANGERS WE [. . .] EACH OTHER*

Hey big sis let's live together just the two of us Don't even bother calling Mom and Dad I think it's really cool to play dead sometimes 'Cause you only look at me when I resort to this The doctor says violence is a good thing Violence is proof that I'm not sick Look! Look at my body I've got athlete's foot The doctor says I'm this red because I'm letting out my anger I want you to be religious I want you to save all your moaning and groaning for that god you like So let's never get married and live together just the two of us Let's lean on each other until we die It'd be super great if we're sisters again in our next life huh? Don't forget I'm the only one who could ever love something like you We're family When I hit your head with the frying pan the other day I did it because I love you Now you know how much I love you Unni I think I have to hit you for you to understand what I'm saying If we can't live together I think we should disappear together Let's die on the same day at the same time Promise your god right now that you'll live and die with me forever Is this something you have to think about? Really you're so weird You have a knack for pissing me off It's like you don't even know how to have a conversation Don't try to patch everything up with a sorry I don't know how you went to college You're so stupid I mean I have to hit you for you to understand what I'm saying Like a little bitch

----

* November 21, 2014: the day Sijin beat me with a frying pan. As a result of those strikes I had the strange experience of briefly seeing double.

A CHURCH WE ERECT TOGETHER

We went to the island

Father always prayed
He slept with a sister at the broken church and
donned his pulpit robe over his already committed sins and
bestowed a blessing upon us

In the name of Sunday, Father forgave
his own secret

Following His will, we brought our hands together and
thought about roofless secrets
We enjoyed eating dead animals on the rooftop after
prayer
Halal, in the name of Allah,
we thought about the IUD loop inside the sister's uterus
We hung a loop even around the sound of her breaths
We could not keep our promise
to protect everything we hung a loop around

Mom and I clipped our fingernails short Flicking misclip-
pings here and there while like a folktale Father's thing turned
into a rat as big as a
forearm Night was day and day was shrouded by night
and Father squeaked quietly under the covers He believed
Squeaksqueak When I lay in the lower bunk Father shook
the bed from up top When Father was shaken the church was

shaken Verse of the day Squeaksqueak No one carried the
cross yet sins were committed

The spangled sins shone even in darkness

I sharpened charcoal and wrote Father's secret I sharpened
the words that are visible here but invisible there I stabbed
Mom with them

Invisible lights shone like spoken words

KYUNGJIN'S HOME
– A STUDIO APARTMENT

My lover wears old sweats with baggy knees and with
even baggier knees I crawl on the floor and cry like spilled
milk My thirtieth year like beer I've popped one bottle more
than him so when I hold the night in my mouth like a dick
it dwindles and when I blow it becomes infinite and when I
cry yet again I become a woman Like a woman I become the
shadow of an offspring The offspring sticks to the callus of
my heels and sucks on me and screeches like a goddamn bird
My lover sucked me off then said my poems suck Said he
heard them and they're
    disgusting

    I rewrite my fully grown lover as Husband

    So I'm telling you Husband
    You should die when you're old

    If you're lucky, you might die of old age
    A fistful of Husband frozen hard in the fridge I try pound-
ing Husband's cheeks against the sink I bang him on the floor

    Why haven't we changed at all?

        Because you keep taking bites out of me you bitch
           Stop shoving food in your big fat mouth
                or stop yapping

Lies

It's because you bastard

keep chomping away at me and everything else in this

apartment

I cut and sell my hair to buy Husband's mouth Husband pokes

through the plastic bag and bites my calf No matter how he

attacks me I

curl my spine while Husband's teeth force my head down Since

his mouth was left open Husband uses it to say my poems

suck To say he's heard them and they're

disgusting I'm chewchewed out like squid while

the bitch

in my stead pops another beer at my husband

KYUNGJIN'S HOME
– MAY 8, PARENTS' DAY

That day it rained like Grandma and
Grandma who tied and cut off her breasts with Dad's tie
became Grandpa and Grandpa
put on the wedding dress cut from a rain poncho and
simply waited for Dad to come

Whether that day brought peaceful death or agonized life

Mom waited for Dad and Dad shaved every head in the
family and offered our hair on the ancestral table It needs to
be an odd number but we're two two four What do we do?
Dad picked up some woman off the street and shaved her
head and sat her down at our table Now we've all gathered
here As Father's Father had become before us we became
baldies with the open mind of bodhisattvas Every time we
sinned the head of the table the head of a ship a head of
lettuce a head of steam ahead of the curve he shaved all heads
Until he reached an odd number he kept chopchopping and
    offering it on the table

Someone was always lonely

Father placed all of our palms on the ceremonial tableware
then hammerhammered the nails in Now we can never
ever part Because we're family Lastly Dad chopped off the
nailhead so it could never be pulled back out

Now you and I have become us

We mixed cooked rice with cold water and ate it up We wrote
our names on hanji paper, slashslashed it up with a fruit knife
to eat, and became written words We embraced each other with
crumpled paper and blackly blackly filled the paper

We were most beautiful when we remained sentences

WITH MOM HANGING FROM MY CROTCH

I covered my carved-up stomach with boxers
I was caught with a crown of bare scalp
Wearing a wig over my frayed hair
I hid Mom in my stomach behind Dad's back

One day Two days with Mom hanging from my crotch
I counted numbers Three days Four days Through the
bladder I stepstepped on for ten months I birthed Mom
leakleaking I raised Mom and fed her and clothed her, while
Dad put his penis in his yellowed boxers and played with
the elastic every night One month Two months

Swelllling

The penis burst open the bladder then the stomach then
what's between the legs

Hush little Mommy

I put burrs of night in Mom's mouth and marinated
Dad's rib in sleep You know it's all for you right Mom? So
don't even make a squeak We were born from Dad's rib
You dozed off on Sunday and missed it again huh? Dad is
sky We are ground Sky ground Star ground

Spitspit

Crumpled like a jujube, I sewed my privates with silk
thread and applied ointment and One month Two months
Ten months Swelllling
  I waited for myself

                    Hey Mom, it's really gross to carry someone
                                              in your stomach
                          It's grossss so don't tell Dad
                                  I'm still a woman

  I ripped off all my goose bumps
  I asked Mom
  Tell me the truth Do I look like a virgin now?

MEDITATION ON FAMILY 1

We
skipskipped
like stones
on water
The chunk of us we couldn't flush
rose
to the surface

KYUNGJIN'S HOME
– A SPIDER WEB

Mom hated bridges
and us strays she'd found under the bridge of her legs

Our ever-cramped cradle
Every night in bed the whole family's legs got tangled
Two times two is four Two four eight
Fuck
That day, Mom birthed 1989 siblings

> *When the sun goes away*
> *the spider climbs its web*

Having only legs we had to live
Whenever we were hungry we practiced tightening our butt-
holes under the covers
With each breath the butthole tightens, the vagina contracts

What a pity Mom's womb grew old and worn after birthing
1989 siblings
Instead of sucking on her teats we injected insulin into her
womb and took turns every day ejaculating between her legs
The ants would swarm every time

Listen up Mom
You're not a woman or anything anymore
You don't laugh even when I lick between your legs like this

Look Look
You can't come even when I stick three fingers inside like this

I shut the door tight

Nineteeneightynine Nineteeneightyeight Nineteeneightyseven
Nineteeneightysix Nineteeneightyfive Nineteeneightyfour
Nineteeneightythree Nineteen, Nineteen, Nineteen

Teen
......Teen......Spleen

Having only legs I
had to live

I ejaculated at Mom The ants swarmed between her legs,
opened their jaws, and pinched her saggy flesh
Mom cried
like a girl who lost her pink nipples at Yeongdeungpo Rotary
as she ripped apart and ate my 1989 siblings swarmed by
blowflies

Rain fell and the web broke
The spider climbs down the web

White fabric and hemp cloth Carbohydrates and chocolate
Maggots and leeches Plus Dad, Dad, Dad of different seeds

I already knew about the abstraction of death

Now

the only way I can talk about myself without mentioning
family

is by making excuses

"Mom always called me a bitch
A mother-eating spider bitch"*

The sun went away and I
spreading all my legs built a home in another branch
A home that even a raindrop could break

---

* Velvet spiders engage in matriphagy, or suicidal maternal care. After
spawning, the mother offers its body as food for its children as an
extreme case of maternal instinct. The children are fated to repeat that
same instinct as they become mothers. One day, Grandmother watched
a documentary on these spiders and cursed at Mom. Called her "a
spider bitch." I remember that day. Like a child Mom locked her door
and wept pitifully.

BLOWFISH SOUP

The day I confessed I wanted to die little sister confessed too.

Have you ever killed anyone?
Don't pretend to be a saint You've had an abortion too huh
You probably even have a cyst in your uterus Dirty bitch

That's why you should've taken your pills every day you
stupid bitch

That day we ate blowfish soup instead of postpartum soup.
We ate in separate rooms. No matter how much I debone it I
feel like the blowfish will be poisonous. We might die. We ate
the funerary soup and shuddered. A few days later maggots
swarmed in the blowfish pot. We ate them up with a ladle.
Listen up. I'm going to die first no matter what. Chewing on
maggots, little sister said,

You've been alive for an awful long time
You're still here Didn't you say you wanted to die?

Don't worry When you die I'm going to die right then

Every night

I covered myself in little sister's skin and stood in front of her
room. Inside I saw little sister wearing a plastic bag on her face.
Little sister choking herself with a belt on a hanger. I saw little

sister dingledangling before my eyes. Erasing the days that
dried up on the bedroom floor, I loosened the belt from the
neck of my swaying sister. I knock.

Knock knock
I'm sorry

The day she confessed she wanted to die I confessed too.

Knock knock
Have you ever killed anyone?
Don't pretend to be a saint You're the dirtiest kind there is

SIJIN'S HOME
– A HOUSE OF DEAD STONES*

We built a house
We built a house with blocks until our fingertips reddened
We built each other's rooms even as we fought off sleep
fearing the blocks would disappear

Leaving my room for last Unni said
You'll leave me

No sis
I even nailed the center stone in the living room for you
Now you just have to nail a no-good pimp with his erect
column here
Don't forget I love you Unni

As I
coaxed and soothed and touched my brother-in-law like Unni

she forgot about the center stone and suffered from herself
and withered away in a corner of the room

Dirty desk chair hair bed and
30 years of weekends of Unni sleeping all day

So as I
coaxed and soothed and touched my brother-in-law like Unni
in her place

he and I played a kind of hopscotch in the living room then
threw a punch at her

Dumbass don't you know there's barely a difference between
the striker and the struck?
So we're not the perps
Stop crying and get up Unni

Unni's still inside the house

We shoved a steel wool pad down her windpipe and listened
to her breathe as she chewchewed through the steel With the
same red hands that built our house we devoured Unni whose
blood was still flowing We left the bones and only ate the flesh
We even ate our red fingers that used to suck on
Unni

Our house made of squares Our square table where we're
squared into us

Like an old lost person with dementia Unni said she didn't
have a house

Stupid bitch

Can you really not remember anything
when we love you this much?

Nobody
Nobody remembered us as the us we used to be

Unni's still inside the house

This us set up two households in the living room and
grabbed a white stone Unni cried as she stacked the leftover
black stone
    We knew even then
    The black stone is always at a disadvantage
    We knew for a fact that all the black stones go
    nowhere[**]

---

[*] In the game of Go, players take turns placing stones on a wooden
board, and the player who builds the most "houses" wins. By the end,
there are often stones that cannot avoid capture but have not yet been
completely surrounded. Usually the two players agree to remove these
"dead stones" as captures.

[**] A player moves their stone to gongbae, the empty space where nei-
ther side benefits or loses, only when there are no other options.

SEPARATION

We combed each other's pubic hair with mascara

The branches of night draped over our legs grew longer and longer

Like lint we are ruined with every touch

As always

Only the words *I love you* were left and we were not

PART 2
THE BIRTH OF THE MOST PERSONAL
AND UNIVERSAL KYUNGJIN

OPPA LIKES THAT TYPE OF GIRL

Whatareyoutryingtosay?Ifyou'refeelingsickgocookyourselfporridge
Whycallme?I'msickofyouYouwannacussmeouthuhGoaheadWhat
areyouafraidof?IgaveyoueverythingbutnothingsatisfiesyouThisis
whyIdon'tlikedepressedgirlsHeystopwhiningandtalkstraightAnd
thinkitoverbeforeyoutalkHaveIbeendatingastupidgirl?That'snotit
You'resmartIcanhaveaconversationwithyouSodon'tactlikeyouknow
somethingIdon'tOppawillexplaineverythingtoyouonebyoneI'm
doingthisallforyouHeyyoudon'tbelieveme?I'mjustkiddingWhyare
youglaringlikethatI'vetoldyoubeforebutit'sbecauseyou'restubborn
andsensitivethatourromanceturnedsourAnyothermanwould've
dumpedyoualreadyI'mlettingyouoffthehookagainDon'tdothisagain
Ifyou'rehavingsuchahardtimedrinkyourselftosleepYou'regoodatthat
You'regoingtoshakeitoffanywayCan'twejusthanguphappynow?I
couldn'tstandtolookatyouroutfitearlierBuyyourselfsomeclothes
whenyougetpaidNotfromanoutletmallbutsomethingbrandname
soyouwon'tfuckingembarrassmeHeyonlyI'dtellyouthisYoucan'tfind
anothermanlikemeanywhereIt'snotthatOppachangedYouchanged
YouusedtoatleastpretendtogetdolledupbutIguessyoudon'teventry
thesedaysAnywayI'mbusyCan'tyouunderstandthat?Ifyoudon'thavea
jobwhydon'tyougetahobbyWatchtvStopwatchingmeIlikeawomanw
ho'sproductiveWhatareyougoingtodowithwhatIdidtodayStopasking
meDoyounottrustme?You'rsoobsessedIfeellikeI'mgoingtolosemy
mindeverytimeyoudothisThisiswhyallthoseguysdumpedyouOnlyI'd
staywithyouallthistimeDon'ttakethisthewrongwayYouthinklovers
can'tsaystufflikethistoeachother?I'mclosertoyouthananyoneelsein
theworldI'mtheonlyonewhothinksofyouDon'tforgetitSobeniceto
yourOppa

I CAN'T READ OR WRITE IN SPANISH*

¿Hablas español? Dijo que hablabas, pero tú no los dijiste. Sólo escucha. Responde correctamente, ¿Por qué no puedes hablar bien? ¿Sabes solamente inglés? ¿No sabes hablar español? Las mujeres orientales no pudieron hablar español, Solamente son idiotas que saben hablar inglés. ¿Tú también eres idiota? Si no es así, ¿me estás diciendo que no entiendes? Eso es muy ridículo. ¡Oye! Me siento mal por eso no puedo conducir más. ¡Si camina por 10 minutos, hay un hotel! ¡Sal de mi taxi! ¡Maldita loca!

---

* Miss, you speak Spanish? Oh, a little? You said you can, aren't you going to talk? You're just listening. Answer me. Why can't you talk right? Do you only speak English? You can't speak Spanish? Asian girls can't speak Spanish. They're idiots who only know English. Are you an idiot too? If that's not it, are you pretending to not understand what I'm saying? Un-fucking-believable. Fuck! You've ruined my mood, I can't drive anymore. Get out here. It's only a ten-minute walk to your hotel! Get out of my taxi! You crazy bitch!

CATCALLING

Heybeautiful Victoria's Secret is snow white Humming
Adóndevas Imagine *DontyouspeakEnglish* Anchovy prince
spit-speaks Dogs go rub-a-dub-dub *Spareaminute* in Central
Park Guns go bang *Chingchangchong* Hopper's windows
All day long *Kissme* Meatball Fat Friday *Quebonita* ABC
Avenue *Hangoutwithme* A ballerina bound by electric wire
Venaquí at midnight A foal-walking class *Gimmeasmilegirl*
lives on as a quote *Youalone* The spring shower waddles
on a tiny island *Drinkwithme* A maze upstairs A hungry
bucket In the middle of the Hudson River *Whatsyournumber*
Soho *Honey* Slaughterhouse *Nicebody* Plane trees *Ilove*
The church tower Whistling all around *Miamor* I took off
my tangled pants *Lookatme* Well-worn pairs of *Hey* hitch-
hikers *Oyemírame* Wet vinyl Vintage lady *Miramesenñorita*
Wannafuck National Police Agency built out of straws
Hellohello China girl crying inside a paper cup A pathway
A shortcut *Areyouignoringme* Going to school with strang-
ers then *Fuckingbitch* dozing off in the corner Mom I'm
fine I'm doing well I'm happy In the meantime my wish is
Gobacktoyourcountry

33

LET US SETTLE[*]

Act I

1887, Whitechapel Police Station in London. JOHNSON and
INSPECTOR 1 and 2 sit with a desk between them. The three
people's hands, a typewriter, a pile of documents, and pencils
are strewn on the desk. INSPECTOR 1 types; INSPECTOR 2 listens.
JOHNSON pulls his hair. Various noises are heard irregularly.

JOHNSON   (Bursting from his seat) I am being wronged! How
is it a sin for a man and a woman to spend a night
together! She must have secretly liked it. That is
why she chose to walk into my home and fall into
my bed. Don't you see?

INSPECTOR 1   (Facing him) Of course.

INSPECTOR 2   Now, now. It would be best for us to leave at
this juncture. Gentlemen don't get involved in the
private lives of others.

INSPECTOR 1   A lover's spat, how sweet!

(Blackout.)

Act II

The main office of a fabric factory. There are two chairs inside
and above them sways an incandescent light bulb. JOHNSON
moves over to the right-side chair. Just then, the sound of a door

opening is followed by those of a machine and footsteps. JOHN-
SON sits up and faces the chair on the left.

JOHNSON   (Looking to his left) Are you really going to say
                 you did not know? After coming over late at
                 night with 'something to say'?

                              (Silence.)

JOHNSON   Sir, do you not recall her saying she is in need of
                 money! Are her motivations not clear as day?

JOHNSON   I shan't speak much. I will fix your problem.
                 (Briefly burying his face in his hands) Will you sit
                 out in the streets, or will you settle?

JOHNSON   Who in London will believe what you say?

                         (A very long pause.)

Several sheets of paper fall to the stage. JOHNSON gathers the
pages and scans them.

JOHNSON   Hark! I am innocent. Hasn't she admitted that
                 too? I am an upstanding citizen!

---

* This play dramatizes the three-month process where Johnson F. Miller,
a capitalist in the Whitechapel District of London, England, was charged
with the rape of his fabric factory employee Alice Smith and subsequently
acquitted. It is based on a Quotidian Courant article from November 25,
1887 titled "The Excessive Force of Female Laborers Towards the Industrial
Bourgeois: The Case of Alice Smith."

THE BIRTH OF THE MOST PERSONAL AND UNIVERSAL KYUNGJIN

"HowsqueakydeandoesshethinksheistomakesuchafussAruglygirlikehershould'veknowntocrawlbackhome"

MISS YOU WHEN I'M TIPSY

Soho, you up? You haven't told anyone about me yet, right? Do you want to take a trip together later? I didn't call to ask you this, I'm just so sad today. Wanna come over? Spend the night with me? I'm in Yeonnamdong, it's a quick taxi ride. Weirdly when I drink I think of you. What it'd be like to date a girl like you, that kind of thing. Nah. Let's not turn into one of those corny couples. Go with the flow. I like you, Soho, because you're chill. Lady artists are different from other girls, you know. You're free. You hate being tied up, just like me. So let's not restrict each other. What's important is that we see eye to eye. Let's meet up and grab some drinks and if we really vibe let's Netflix and chill. Hey, what do you mean, "What are we?" What does that have to do with anything. You and I, we're grown-ups. What in the world is your definition of dating? A man and a woman getting together regularly and having fun and eating and fucking. That's what we're doing right now. Can only people in relationships do that? I still don't understand what your problem is. Women are so weird. They spend time with you just fine then pull this shit. Whatever, you've ruined my day. You don't know how to accept us as we are.

HOLIDAY PARTY

You know I read a lot of debut collections these days.
Listen, being a poet means going crazy. You need to go one
step farther from where you are right now. Make the read-
ers kneel at your feet. Kill all your literary heroes and jump
over our dead bodies. Yeah, you write good poems. If you
weren't any good I wouldn't even bother saying this. But I
think you're stuck in a rut writing about your family. Since
you don't seem to understand, I'll give you an example.
Who's your favorite poet? That's right, you said you wanted
to be like Choi Seungja, but you can't become Choi Seungja.
Because you're different. The only Choi Seungja in the world
is Choi Seungja herself. Your poems are like, how do I say
this. They haven't reached the edge? You could go farther.
I'm saying, you need to be much more extreme than you
are now. I'll give you an example of a poet who went there.
That's right, Choi Seungja.

The way I see it, it's because you're nice but you act like
you're not. If you think that's really you, stick with it! Like
a crazy bitch. I'm telling you, hang on the edge of poetry.
Then take another step forward from there. Tell me, which
poet are you going to fight and win against? Who do you
think you can compete with? Your poetry, to be honest,
can't beat anyone yet.

APOLOGY LETTER

Hello, I am Lee Soho and I write poems.

First, I would like to apologize for troubling my readers who have shown me love. I made a mistake under the pressure to keep producing new work and survive the literary establishment. In particular, I hadn't considered how certain readers could be hurt by something I'd written without much thought. I thought that any sentence was admissible within the frame of poetry. With this lesson as my springboard, I will avoid provocative words in the future and think deeply before I act. I will try my hardest to compensate for this literary mistake with better literature.

Thank you.

PART 3
THE ISLAND BACK THEN

THE ISLAND BACK THEN

Night after night I hear a rustle

The bed in our house is lonely

Giant canvas

Dead cockscomb and mobile sculpture

Birches

trapped in an old matchbox

unaware of each other's heads shattering

like flints

Doomed we were silent

The forest inside the mirror

grew thick all winter long

Glow in the dark stars sparkle

Raindrops scatter on the meek eaves

The back I faced was familiar and fearsome

I

became a useless drawing

DELUSION BEACH

A couple on the beach built a sand castle on each other's
faces. The waves rolled in like a ringtone and pushed out
their footprints. Wanting to be rescued from my own foot-
prints I waved my hands. We who've walked the waves. We
who are still worth less than the styrofoam in the boundless
open sea. Because he was a swim tube, because I was a tube
that wouldn't inflate no matter how much I was blown and
blown, we couldn't even sink.

We lay under the massive colorful umbrella to avoid the
sun. While he strummed the guitar and sang a song worth
less than the trash he'd collected I was still sprawled out like
an empty bottle pinned mouth-first. The beach is where sand
gathers grain by grain but can never coalesce. A place where
we hold hands and shout *Neverhavelever* but never learn
names. I walked lovingly with a pair of slippers that delusion
wore then threw away. Sharing bites of each other from
the spot where the breakwater stands tall to the plastic mat
where the wind blows sand into our mouths.

HYEHWA DISTRICT

I talk about you who's like me Like a cat that climbs into
every hole you dig I talk about the I that is you Clothes
hangers hold up the February days that fall short On the
other end of the phone that I've crossed wearing white
socks boiled clean, the words I left behind are shivering Like
diaries stacked on dust Like toes that couldn't cross the door
threshold I am shivering having gone farther than myself

I am from you

I have fewer words than the long strand of hair laid on
your bed We flip words and watch their backs The back
of a day, the back of a toothbrush, the back of a slice of
cranberry bread, the back of a Mickey Mouse T-shirt, and
the back of an island You are lonely like a clipped fingernail
Island, Island I turn off the switch and think of a darkened
lighthouse

BAMSEOM*

Feelings finally exposed by a chewed-up fingernail

A single raindrop fell

I

like a shoulder ousted from an umbrella

was soaked

---

* A pair of uninhabited islets in the Han River

ROOSEVELT ISLAND

Carrying shade on my back inside
the light,

I want to smoke hookah with you on the island. I want
to order wine by the glass and tell you about poetry. Then
you'd look into my eyes and talk about paintings. About
Cézanne who mixes multiple perspectives. About your eyes
lighting up when you talk about Cézanne, I'd probably
write. The black bed and a cup and a white rose trapped in a
narrow canvas. A country that straps a bra on us. Then we'd
probably say why this moment is grand. We'd go from island
to island and lie around. Away from prying eyes we'd sit in
your room and gaze at Manhattan. Tomorrow let's go to
Grand Central and eat Junior's cheesecake. Let's eat it over a
Wong Kar Wai movie. Let's listen to Lang Lee. Let's not get
caught. Then we'd probably laugh at ourselves for being so
pathetic. We'd drape the curtain around our necks and stand
in front of the mirror and say we look great together. We
love each other this much, how is this not love?

We'd laugh

It snowed a lot the day I went back, you said. Nobody in
New York could leave their house, you said.

SHANGHAI, WHERE YOU DON'T LIVE

Your drawing's too small A twisted donut crying in a
squat in front of the station A warty sea squirt splattered
inside a western toilet I drew a house You drew an estuary a
dock A new world that digs up and eats Waitan and rubber
boots and old side dishes and a grandfather clock. A bridge
brought over to a city torn apart That was our little island
We gnawed at each other under the lemon tree soaked in
acid rain but didn't know how to kill Walks were always
exhausting for no reason We walked from a distant place
toward an even more distant place Only after being hung on
each of our own walls could we see each other The spectacle
of blue soap bubbles popping on your palm Pigeons rubbing
their faces inside a dirt hole My face hanging upside down
reflected on the mercury-coated windowpane. I rub my head
on a flaming frame Tones and rhythm April when we were
wetted by breaths and died in the swelter like dumplings like
socialists The portrait you drew with nails over a shipwreck
in the estuary the dock you drew Duìbùqǐ It was a dirty trip
Two people who are now disappeared and gone from the
island. The night: inscribes the umbrella* The umbrella: rips
the night A hostel built without embankments by plasterers
planting plantains in the trunk Cotton blankets pouring
from the nacre wardrobe The matter of watching alone in
a double bed: the public square where people who tore off

---

* It is said that even in heavy rain, Chinese lovers do not use umbrellas
together because they believe, following the pronunciation, that 伞 (san,
umbrella) will end in 散 (san, scatter).

their flesh walk lawless The matter of dying: from being hit with
knife-marked rocks We could draw only after we were thrown out
to a distant world

A DISAPPEARED PERSON AND A FOREST THAT DIDN'T DISAPPEAR OR THE OPPOSITE OF THAT*

You write

Under the sunlight where a tree wider than a wingspan
shattershatters
    you make me walk alone on paper. You write there an island, a
forest, trees, legless chairs, clam shells whose traps don't close, a
bird that fell alone while building a
    flock At the bottom of the page you
    buy a handful of periods and

again
I am written
as a such and such person
who is so used
to meeting over coffee over beer in bed

A character's supposed to be dimensional
What's bad about changing?

I opened some quote marks
and cried only in your sentences

"A good person. A good person. Still a good person."

Like laundry stiffened and sprawled on the floor
I am tossed and wrinkled whichever way to be worn at random

Your nude body just as it is I

wordlessly watch sadness lose its rhythm

as we who dive into each other's eyes

now

go to a world where we sometimes say hi but never know how
each other's doing

Two minus one is zero

Absolutely nothing

So I am written. Soho, don't look at the tree, see the forest.
Try coloring it in. The hours you kneaded like dough then plop-
plopped by force: try drawing them. An eye that's far far away, a
hand, a back to be placed even farther than that: imagine them.
A night just for the two of us, covered in black oil pastel. Look
closely, let's carve out a world of our own over there with this
paperclip

Doesn't this cheer you up?

We walked through a forest black like charcoal
Following closely behind you I sometimes
place my chest
against your heart
that I accidentally

cut out with a paperclip

Then I move away

It's cold

* Derived from the title of Cha Mihye's film *Disappeared Characters and a World That Didn't Disappear or the Opposite of That*

52

PRACTICE

When time makes space for us to grab lunch sometime we lose our body heat at last. Your dear palm like the last leaf between dense trunks. Days left over from slashing one by one with our fingers interlocked. When we met up again we bared our skin on a porcelain plate: half your profile stacked on half the back of my head. With gratitude for every moment we say grace for the repose of the dead. For the things that must come to naught according to the Holy Will we once enjoyed. Naked like the day we re-re-relive we get motion sickness while the sound of confessions leaving the room still rings in our ears. After recounting the life I shared with you and playing the last note comes the way back to the start. You returned with me to the bitter end; I'll practice nonchalance for when I realize I'd been forgotten long ago. Please just don't get caught with the lie du jour.

REFLECTOR*

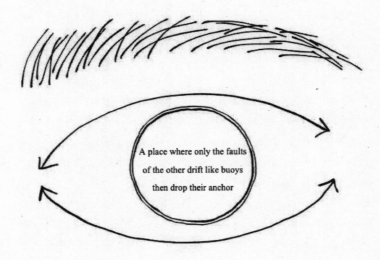

A place where only the faults
of the other drift like buoys
then drop their anchor

---

* Lee Soho's words placed inside a drawing by webtoon artist Ha Yangji.

PART 4
KYUNGJINMUSEUM OF MODERN ART

ENCOUNTER*

This is your last chance
to turn back

1 minute
He said

Kyungjin, thanks to you
I think I can become a good person

There's no such thing as a good person Like a horse
the words became a son of a bitch as soon as the reins
came off Not even

1 minute

since talking shit in a tiny room in Siheungdong I
embraced the son of a bitch Pollen flurried outside the
window Oppa's cough slapped my cheek I shook the flower
branch I shook it madly so that buds of Oppa's spit would
spray across my cheek

1 minute

Open your eyes and listen up, Kyungjin
Jazz follows the bass rhythm Just like that I
followed the footprints left by the bass It sucks Oppa I
don't understand the bass no matter how much I listen I just
like blowing I like blowing with others You know trumpet,

saxophone
    That sort of thing
    1 minute

    Beat by beat, we listened to jazz and built the Great Wall
of China, in the middle of which we decided to meet Oppa
carried the bass and I blew the saxophone We braided our
legs into a single strand We crossed the bed on one foot

    Yeah! This is what I call jamming

    1 minute

    We carved sharp rocks and built another Great Wall of
China in the middle of the
    bed Building a stone tower in every crevice, we made
wishes laden with expletives

If only I'd found a sharper rock first
                    I would've struck your head and killed you first

    Oppa, tell me Is this what you call jamming?

    1 minute

    Doobee doobop ptooey, ptooey, ptooey
    Kyungjin died carving up the last rock
    Kyungjin used to get spanked with drumsticks, play only
the black keys on the piano, and scat When she

died, Oppa said

1 minute

        Soho, please don't go anywhere else now

1 minute

To Kyungjin whom he once dated

        Oppa said

        This is your last chance
        to turn back

1 minute**

---

* *An Encounter with Marina Abramovic* is the translated Korean title of *The Artist Is Present*, a performance where Abramovic sits across from a stranger and they look into each other's eyes silently for a minute. Her former longtime artistic collaborator and romantic partner Ulay visited her for the first time in decades and participated in her performance. They, like all the others, looked at each other silently for a minute before he left.

** The encounter goes on.

MAMAN*

Instead of a womb
I was born from a pile of red thread
As Dad was threading between bitches he believed were his fate
Mom's needle hole grew bigger
and those bitches' holes grew smaller

> We're growing toward death
> Follow His words and have faith

Strands slipped from Dad's fingertips
Mom cried hanging her neck on the strand loosened
above his groin and tied the cross with thread Mom
prayed with the cross shoved up between her legs

> Baby, believe in God when you're lonely
> Everyone who believes in God is kind

What about Dad?
> Your daddy loves everyone If that's a sin that's
> his

Trying to measure the scale of faith
Mom kneeled and crawled as far as Dad's sole
Conversation broke off like columnar joints

While Mom was transforming from Mary Magdalene into the
Virgin Mary

I squinted hard as if peering through the eye of a needle
at us
at the palmistry fate line extended in the name of family
at the two hands that put the fate lines together in prayer every
dawn

Now we're growing toward Heaven
Follow His words and have faith

Mom was suckling Dad when he bit her

Secret room, red room, no exit**

April 4, Holy Week
Our Heavenly Father's words are in bloom again today Like
the wind I tried to bloom my buds as a Messiah For I love every-
one For I loved every church sister

April 5, Easter Sunday
Bloom your flowers, Father, for you love me Only love and care
about me as the days you sucked Mary's supple breasts

With a needle Mom mended Dad's words
Mom ripped off Dad's hair and stitched it back Mom raised
Dad Mom suckled Dad Mom erected Dad's pillar until her tongue
wore out Now all of Dad's words are faint

I loved our family If that's a sin that's
mine

The needle grew as much as the house

So did the door and the windows In the dark

like the inside of a secret room Mom hooked several more

crochet needles on her fingers and

made all those bitches and Dad wear a red sweater tight

around the neck

Inside the red room, Dad laughed twisting his limbs

I stole glimpses of Dad fooling around with those bitches

There,

pushing between a pair of pillows

raising her needles

Mom said

> Don't hate him too much
> Daddy is everyone's father
> just like Our Heavenly Father

---

* Louise Bourgeois was a French-born American abstract expressionist sculptor. She earned international acclaim after the age of 70 as the "godmother" of contemporary art. Her best known work, *Maman*, depicts a giant spider.

** Artist Lee Kyungjin of KOMA said of *Maman*, "I've borrowed only the keywords 'needle,' 'maternity,' and 'red room' from Louise Bourgeois' numerous works. That's all. Full disclosure, this is not the story of Louise Bourgeois. It is merely a very personal story of mine."

SONG OF GREATEST TURBULENCE*

He made me swallow the musical notes first
Before my husband ate me
I walked the desert stuck between a camel's budding humps
Your hair's so soft
His hand reached in between
and stroked my hair
With a glare the night
was crossing over my husband

Oh oh a cramped ceremonial bow toward my husband's crotch

I had no choice but to bend my knees
Instead of moans we only spoke in ellipses
Responses always in periods
.

                                        When I want to sing
                                          I cross the desert
                                  to the island of Manhattan

                                  Holding a fork and knife I
                                      cut a slice of pork
                    on a pixelated plate in Madison Square Garden
                            This little piggy drenched in blood
                        and azure blue cyan glass shards went in
                                  jumbled onto the tongue

A prayer to my husband
I'll even tweeze the hairs out so it'll be nice for you to eat
I won't pester you like a piggy
Covering my face in dry lettuce you
bite me and swallow

When I want to sing a different song
I place my husband up on the hump and write over and over
again my name

Kyungjin, Kyungjin, Kyungjin
Kyungjin I don't want to eat anymore
Not your sagging tits, not even your protruding nipples
I don't want to eat you dirty bitch

Named obedience, my mouth and ears were cut off

Yet I perform a cramped ceremonial bow toward my husband
*Yalali yallahsung yalali yallah**
with your second and third wives
hidden in bed

When I want to sing a completely different song I
ask Do you believe in me
Do you believe in God This is the era of conversions
Do you believe in me Do you really
Can you swear in front of God that you believe in me
Of course, God, of course I kill it In bed I mean
Then you'll say Oh God, God damn
it! Eat! Eat!

A prayer to my husband
I say this with my legs wrapped around you
How's this I'm better than God huh
You know I've always been this bitch
You believe in me don't you?

---

* The adjective "greatest/most" in Korean is homonymous with the noun "head of household" as well as the verb "to pretend." This poem, though prompted by the ban on Iranian women singing in public as depicted in Iranian artist Shirin Neshat's video *Turbulent*, is not a statement on Islam.

** The chorus of "Cheongsanbyeolgok" (Song of the Green Mountains), a folk song from the Goryeo dynasty (918–1392). These words have no meaning but are sung in tune with the melody.

STRANGE DEATH OF NANA*
– PAINT AND VARIOUS OBJECTS

I hung the testicles behind the canvas
I drew a house a room walls corners
I drew them all I trapped myself inside
I inflated Dad his testicles then I
bared my ass and felt his paternal love I let
myself feel it Like that I pointed the gun

WHITE FRIDAY

Dad sculpted the bed from plaster and smashed it with a hammer
We ate the shattered bed, the sharp bed together Embracing
each other night after night like lovers

we prayed
You're not going to have another child, are you?

Our house, known as a random abstraction,
is an elaborate reality

Dad couldn't help himself and again
had Na^{2**} My twin Na^2 with breasts as big as a butt It's fun to
play with all sorts of Na^2 always
Zero zero seven bang bang bang***
Everyone screaming is "it"
Lalala
It's fun because Na^2's blood is rainbow-colored

RAINBOW FRIDAY

I spread plastic between my legs I planted Na^2 I didn't even miss
my lunar cycle I fed her well so her belly would swell
    like a burial mound We were squatting leakleaking on the easel
when Dad said

                              I wish for all of us to flow together
                                              like a movie

BLOODY FRIDAY

Now
our house, known as an elaborate reality,
is a contrived abstraction

                                          Like a famous painting
                    the first transparent canvas I ever got to have

Silent screams
Silent pointing
Silent
Zero zero seven bang

BLACK FRIDAY

I drew an already torn house on the canvas
    I drew the corners There I trap Dad who didn't know how to
close his
    zipper I trapped him forever

A war, a bloodless murder, an innocent murderer only Dad
didn't know about
Because we're family Because I'm
forever his
kid I wordlessly
bared my ass and felt his paternal
love with my whole body Because we're family I wordlessly
pointed the gun at Dad
and shouted

[Zero zero seven]
Bang!

---

* Niki de Saint Phalle, a French sculptor, started making art to treat the
sexual violence she suffered from her father in childhood. This poem was
inspired by Niki de Saint Phalle's life, her work *Strange Death of Gambrinus*, and her method of "shooting painting."

** The twin of "Nana," the mascot of happiness made by Niki de Saint
Phalle. "Na" means "I" in Korean. The second-person I. I to the second
power.

*** A Korean drinking game for large groups where participants mime
shooting and being shot. The more advanced version of this game is conducted silently.

KYUNGJIN RECLINING*

I saw her

for the first time I snuck a peek at Kyungjin** in the mirror

slanted on the ceiling I twisted her neck along the pillow's edge

and said

Look up bitch Look straight bitch You gotta look at the sky to

pick the stars

I strangled Kyungjin and asked

Feel good?

Night, I could only light up my desires I didn't know darkness

We picked a pile of stars

When I laid Kyungjin under the stars I was so happy I wept

with my dick

Kyungjin comforted me as I cried

Holding me

in her mouth she asked

How come only you get to feel good?

Dummy you must not know since it's your first time but

you don't say I love you with words

I'll show you with my actions

I can love up to five times in one night

Instead of answering Kyungjin shut her own trap

to write stage directions with her left hand and dialogue with her

right She wrote

about the day she was more embarrassed by her mismatched
bra and panties than
her legs spread apart
She wrote about the day I just blamed her big hole
not knowing jack shit, not realizing I was thin and slim
down there

*Kyungjin: (Jumping out of bed) Yeah, I'm asking 'cause
it's my first time and I don't really know but (Beat) is it sup-
posed to feel good only for you the whole time?*

We grew short
in one breath

---

* Sylvia Sleigh often draws male nudes. By subverting the male gaze, she
exposes the various violences and sexism to which women are subjected
on canvas throughout Western art history. Sleigh's works include *Philip
Golub Reclining*.

** The first boyfriend of artist Lee Kyungjin whose work is on display at
Kyungjinmuseum of Modern Art (KOMA). Lee revealed that she suffered
from ego-fragmentation, separation anxiety, depression, and other forms
of psychological anguish while dating someone with the same name and
that it became an inspiration for her art.

EVERY MAN WHO HAS RIDDEN AND WRITTEN ME[*]

to Kyungjin

You're having a hard time these days because of me huh
I know It's because of the guilt It's because of the girl I used
to see She returned my long-lost happiness to me She's the
one I liked so much you were jealous After we broke up
she started attending brothels instead of classes and selling
her body and bumping lips to earn money for a plane ticket
I knew it when I randomly saw her at the bus station. I
thought of her changed appearance before I thought of you.
It tortured me Kyungjin I feel this way the nicer you are to
me or the happier I am But I don't want to lose you How
selfish am I? I don't expect understanding and forgiveness
I'm just frustrated. I just don't want to hide it. Lovers should
always be honest anyway I'm sorry and I've been sorry. But
know that I'm trying I think it's really hard to be happy It
occurred to me that you could leave me. Now my job is
to cheer you up from being disappointed after reading this
letter I'll try harder I don't think I've said this to you recently
It's a little awkward to say under these circumstances but I
love you my dear

January 3, 2010
from Kyungjin[**]

to Kyungjin

You're having a hard time these days because of me huh I
know It's because of the guilt It's because of the girl I used to

see She returned my long-lost happiness to me She's the one
I liked so much you were jealous Kyungjin I feel this way the
nicer you are to me or the happier I am But I don't want to
lose you How selfish am I? I don't expect understanding and
forgiveness I'm just frustrated. I just don't want to hide it.
Lovers should always be honest anyway I've been sorry. But
know that I'm trying I think it's really hard to be happy I'll
try harder

January 30, 2010
from Kyungjin

to Kyungjin
  You're having a hard time these days because of me huh
I know It's because of the girl I used to see She returned my
long-lost happiness to me She's the one I liked so much you
were jealous Kyungjin I feel this way the nicer you are to me
or the happier I am But I don't want to lose you I just don't
want to hide it. Lovers should always be honest But know
that I'm trying

February 3, 2010
from Kyungjin

to Kyungjin
  You're having a hard time these days because of me huh
I know it's because of the girl I used to see She returned
my long-lost happiness to me I don't want to hide it Lovers
should always be honest

March 1, 2010
from Kyungjin

to Kyungjin
You're having a hard time these days because of me huh.
I know

March 2, 2010
from Kyungjin

---

* Tracey Emin, the queen of confession and the most polarizing artist in England, is famous for exhibiting herself as she is. Through collage, drawing, installations, and more, she expresses her life as a work of art. Her works include *Everyone I Have Ever Slept With 1963–1995*.

** For the record, this is an actual letter that the author Lee Kyungjin received while dating Min Kyungjin. Accordingly, the copyright holder of this poem is not the author, but Mr. Min.

I walked to the ends of the earth

I should put the dot here I bet

I walked the southern style In what's left
of the season, the wrung neck of October
I forget you My sharpened pencil crosses out the con-
gested passage of you as the book long left open shuts its
mouth again

My panties are wet and I feel empty inside

Can I do it? Can I do it now?

You walked the northern style You
straightened your toes and took small steps
You picked up a wingless bird and stuck it to the ground
You pecked at my bottom and
plucked off my lips In the pouring dark

we carved our flesh jostling against each other like waves
of a shallow sea

I wasn't lonely because I was alone

I was lonely because we were us

Just as we endure the tides by dividing their ebb and flow
you wash my hands and I yours
and hide them in our panties

I should put the dot here I bet

Can I do it now

Tears prop up my eyes and look at you

From the start it was just the two of us
Me and the gap in between

---

* Derived from the title of Cheon Kyeongja's *Page 22 of My Sorrowful Legend*.

PART 5
ARCHIVE FOR 31 VERSIONS OF LEE KYUNGJIN

SOUTHBOUND FROM SEOUL FOR EIGHT HOURS
AND FIVE MINUTES

Hey Sijin
When did we start playing with scars?

It's only fair that we get 'em from fighting

Life is hell
Peace is surreal

Southern and northern hemispheres
We become each other's patient

"A game of chicken enjoyed on the equator"

Unni you better watch your mouth.
Heard you've been talking shit about me

I heard that rumor too

Little sister grabbed an axe and chopped off my scarlet
military boots and dyed herself the same and I
cried in an awkward squat

Now that you've lost a leg you
won't be able to walk or crawl
You're basically left to be attacked

With an amputated leg I hopped around My fights became leg-
endary and were passed around from mouth to mouth and grew
dirty and jumped over the corpse of a fellow soldier Sijin buried
a massive bomb in the ground and caused trouble and closed her
eyes Three two one bang!

"Cocaine from Cairns $300 a gram"

Unni listen close We've grown addicted
I'm gonna blow off
our heads so we can never go back home

Shootshoot
Bangbang

"There's no revolution or comrade for a traitor"

Above the firing squad

I'm dancing a hanghanging
dance and the dance is
dancing me

Tie me tighter I don't want to wander anymore

I know
Mom and Dad must've abandoned us No surprise there
What's the point in telling you Unni You abandoned me too

Because we happen to be alive

Because we can't stop taking aim

We were sad

We
made up justifications to aim and shoot
at each other's ear holes 'cause we were busy

"Eat breakfast eat lunch finally eat dinner then BANG!"

Now who wants to count and see who has more lines on her
wrist?

I see you're a sergeant about to retire I'm only a private

How many nights must we exchange
blows to see stars?

"Dear Heavenly Father
Just as we've forgiven those who've wronged us
please forgive our sins"

We prayed for each other's victories
Smiling hashishfully and
dancing twirlswirl
again

Unni do you finally understand
how many kinds of love there are in the world?
Saint Peter loved Jesus too

I'll confess

I love you

So let's never come alive again Let's never wake again Let's
never open our eyes again Let's never even wave our panties Let's
never surrender or give up ever again Let's not be mousy Let's
not cry Let's neither catch nor get caught Let's never ever see each
other alive Whoever falls over and dies

wins

DRAWING A SINGLE BOUNDARY

Squatting by a telephone pole I

piss on your turf

A fistful of pills

A face copied with pencil lead

Like sleeping in

Hi I'm

back home

NARROW, EVEN MORE CRAMPED, AND RATHER CONCISE

Even

if a merry

place beckons me

my only place of rest is a

modest home my home Only my

home my shining home is where I can rest

like a broken piano key Love my home my merry

family There's no place like home I won't forget the dream

I laid out on the horizon painting my windows in the evening

Dear clear wind where is the spring day Where I cry one two they open

their eyes together Home sweet home sweet friend There's no place like home*

What'stheproblemSpititoutWhat'ssohardthatyouneedtogoseeashrinkLookat

yourmomanddadAslongasyousteelyourselfyoucanovercomeanythingHeyhoney

whyareourdaughtersinsane?WetreatthemsowellTheydon'tmakemoneyorhelp

aroundthehouseThey'rejustghostseatingupourmoneyTheyalwayssaythey'resick

asifweshouldbeimpressedIhavenoideawhytheykeeplosingtheirshitIhearother

people'skidsdon'tevensayathinginfearthattheirparentswouldworrybutoureldest

daughteryapsonandonabouteverylittlethingWhatsinhaveIcommittedtobepunished

likethisI'msicktodeathofitallOncetheyhavetheirownkidsthey'llrealizehowhard

itwasfortheirmomanddadandfeelremorseWait'tilyouhaveadaughterjustlike

youandspendallyourdayssupportingheruntilshe'sthirtyDon'tcometouswhen

shemakesafussaboutartorwhateverandquitsherofficejobexactlylikeyouYouknow

inmynextlifeIwanttobebornasKyungjin'schildorKyungjinHowhappyIwouldbe

We'resogoodtoherHush!Don'ttalkbacktoanadultWhenyouactlikeabitch

we'retheoneswhogetblamedFromnowonwhenadultspeakjustacceptit

Don'teventhinkJustsayyesyesIunderstandandnothingelseGot it?Answerme!

---

* A variation on Kim Jae-in's adaptation of Henry Bishop's song "Home, Sweet Home."

SONG OF UTMOST FILIAL PIETY

YESYESYESYESYESYESYESYESYESYESYESYESYESYESYESYESYESYESYESYESYESYESYESYESYESYES
YESYESYESYESYESYESYESYESYESYESYESYESYESYESYESYESYESYESYESYESYESYESYESYESYESYES
YES**YESYES**YESYESYESYES**YESYES**YES**YESYESYESYESYESYES**YES**YESYESYESYESYESYES**YESYES
YES**YESYES**YESYESYESYES**YESYES**YES**YESYESYESYESYES**YESYES**YES**YESYESYESYESYES**YESYES
YESYES**YESYES**YESYES**YESYES**YESYESYES**YESYES**YESYESYESYES**YESYES**YESYESYESYESYES
YESYESYES**YES**YESYES**YES**YESYESYESYES**YESYES**YESYESYESYESYES**YESYES**YESYESYESYESYES
YESYESYES**YESYESYESYES**YESYESYESYES**YESYES**YESYESYESYESYES**YESYES**YESYESYESYESYES
YESYESYESYES**YESYESYESYESYESYES**YESYESYESYES**YESYESYESYES**YESYESYESYESYES**YESYES**YESYES
YESYESYESYES**YESYES**YESYESYESYESYES**YESYESYESYESYES**YESYESYESYES**YESYESYESYES**YESYES
YESYESYESYES**YESYES**YESYESYESYESYES**YES**YESYESYESYESYESYESYESYESYESYES**YESYES**YESYES
YESYESYESYES**YESYES**YESYESYESYESYES**YES**YESYESYESYESYESYESYESYESYES**YESYES**YESYES
YESYESYESYES**YESYES**YESYESYESYESYES**YES**YESYESYESYESYESYESYESYES**YESYES**YESYES
YESYESYESYES**YESYES**YESYESYESYESYES**YESYESYESYESYES**YES**YES**YESYESYESYESYES**YESYES**YESYES
YESYESYESYES**YESYES**YESYESYESYESYES**YESYESYESYESYES**YESYESYESYES**YESYESYESYESYES
YESYESYESYESYESYESYESYESYESYESYESYESYESYESYESYESYESYESYESYESYESYESYESYESYESYES
YESYESYESYESYESYESYESYESYESYESYESYESYESYESYESYESYESYESYESYESYESYESYESYESYESYES
MOMMOMMOMMOMMOMMOMMOMMOMMOMMOMMOMMOMMOMMOMMOMMOMMOMMOMMOMMOMMOMMOM
MOMMOMMOMMOMMOMMOMMOMMOMMOMMOMMOMMOMMOMMOMMOMMOMMOMMOMMOMMOMMOMMOM
MOM**MOM**MOMMOMMOMMOM**MOM**MOM**MOMMOMMOM**MOM**MOMMOMMOMMOMMOMMOM**MOM**MOM
MOM**MOMMOM**MOMMOMMOM**MOMMOM**MOM**MOMMOMMOMMOM**MOM**MOMMOMMOMMOM**MOMMOM**MOM
MOM**MOMMOMMOM**MOM**MOMMOMMOM**MOM**MOMMOMMOM**MOM**MOM**MOMMOMMOM**MOMMOM**MOM
MOM**MOMMOMMOM**MOMMOMMOM**MOM**MOMMOMMOMMOM**MOM**MOM**MOMMOM**MOMMOM**MOMMOM
MOM**MOM**MOMMOM**MOM**MOMMOMMOM**MOM**MOMMOMMOMMOMMOMMOM**MOM**MOMMOM**MOM
MOM**MOM**MOMMOM**MOM**MOMMOM**MOM**MOMMOMMOMMOM**MOM**MOMMOMMOMMOM**MOM**MOM
MOM**MOM**MOMMOMMOMMOM**MOM**MOM**MOMMOMMOM**MOM**MOMMOMMOMMOMMOM**MOM**MOM
MOM**MOM**MOMMOMMOMMOM**MOM**MOMMOMMOMMOM**MOM**MOMMOMMOMMOMMOM**MOM**MOM
MOM**MOM**MOMMOMMOMMOM**MOM**MOM**MOMMOMMOM**MOM**MOMMOMMOMMOMMOM**MOM**MOM
MOM**MOM**MOMMOMMOMMOM**MOM**MOM**MOMMOM**MOM**MOM**MOMMOMMOM**MOM**MOMMOMMOMMOM**MOM**MOM
MOMMOMMOMMOMMOMMOMMOMMOMMOMMOMMOMMOMMOMMOMMOMMOMMOMMOMMOMMOM
MOMMOMMOMMOMMOMMOMMOMMOMMOMMOMMOMMOMMOMMOMMOMMOMMOMMOMMOMMOM

MAY I LIVE WITH SOUTH-FACING WINDOWS
IN MY NEXT LIFE, PLEASE

Soho, it's your Mom calling. Daerim's no place to live since a bunch of Chinese people moved there. You heard right? Someone died just a few days ago. He was stabbed and they don't know why. He was killed by a stranger, that's the worst part. It didn't happen somewhere else, it was Seoul. It's so hard to live in Korea as a Korean. I don't understand it one bit. There are so many houses. Oh by the way, do you know about Hangdong? No, not Hwangdong, of course it makes sense you don't know but it's also not that far from here. It's in Seoul but people don't realize it's in Seoul. It's hard to walk from the station so you have to take a local bus but the building is still new. If you don't like it then there's Doosan Apartment that's over 20 years old, right across the street from us. There's nothing else. Over there they've got rust and cockroaches. Plus redevelopment will be tough from the looks of it. You're just buying a giant slab of concrete so you can say you live in the center of Seoul

From line 2 to line 9 From line 9 to line 5 From line 5 to line 1

Then how about Gwangmyeong? Gwangmyeong's practically Seoul you know. Remember that apartment we saw crossing the bridge when we lived in Geumcheon-gu? That's Gwangmyeong. The area code's 02 and those neighborhoods you talk about all the time from Dangsan to Mullaedong or Yeongdeungpo-gu Office are trendy and expensive. You just don't know. I want to live there too, just give me the money. How nice it would be for me. Get a place somewhere like Dangsandong, so what if it's a little chilly? It'll face north but I'll see the Han River. Ugh I'm so sick of facing west. Each day is so long when we see the sunlight all day. Don't say you're tired of it. Do you know how hard it is to move every two years? If you add this and that to the real estate brokerage commission then you're out 2,000,000₩ easy. What do you figure out on your own? Your mom does it all for you. We're all just trying to live but I still don't understand why you want to stay in Seoul. How much longer do you need to live the city life, Soho? I was born and raised in Seoul but I don't know if Seoul's all that great. Seriously

DRIED YELLOW CORVINA, PICKLED VEGETABLES, AND DYSTOPIA

We wore old sweats with baggy knees and dried out in our tiny room Mom yanked hard harder on the belt around our necks We used only five squares of toilet paper for poop and flushed only after everyone peed This goddamn house

KYUNGJIN'S HOME
– A GAME OF TOAD HOUSE*

It passes through the night The room
passes through that night and in that room
Daddy's little girl Mommy's Daddy's little girl Daddy's Daddy's
little girl
These little bitches pass through Dad
Fapfap Daddy sweeps the floor then lies down

Dad put Mom's head under the threshold and built a toad
house for her
He waited

for the tide to rise

Wifey, you know we'll be better off if we stamp a lucky mole
right here Dad stamped a mole between Mom's eyebrows The
mole grew bigger Bigger than her pupils Covering her entire body
until she couldn't breathe anymore We quieted our breaths toward
Mom who had a lucky mole stamped between her eyebrows and
starved
to death

The sea set out for far away and did not return

We sang rounds with the soles of our feet and performed a
ritual for the gods of the earth We grasped our hungry stomachs
and stamped another lucky mole between Dad's eyebrows too

We placed a single sweetbrier under the pillow and
crunchcrunched on raw rice behind the folding screen

Dad flipped the dining table

                                        Hapless bastard

We with our palms spread wide open hit Dad on the back
of his head We wrapped his neck in bedsheets and waited
for the rising tide We stamped Dad's mole whenever we were
hungry We stamped it every day with our fists Like Mom
we put his head in the toad house and put him to sleep

Now every night for Dad
no matter how much he sleepsleepsleeps is night

Mud filled his mouth

---

* A Korean folk game for children where they put their hand inside wet
sand or dirt and build a "house" around it. They pat the dirt singing,
"Toadie, toadie, I'll give you an old house, please give me a new house"
and try to remove their hand without breaking the house of dirt.

MY LITTLE DIARY
— OUR HOME

April 6, 1987
I made a child

Outside the house

I cut off my balls with a kitchen knife

and lowered my pants

Look closely Sijin

A child is something you make together

You can make it with your eyes closed now

Now that you've done it once

you can also do it indoors right?

MY LITTLE DIARY
– KYUNGJIN'S HOME

February 19
I wore baby clothes and a bridal veil
Little sister and I were stuck on top of the same wedding cake
Single room, we spared our words in bed

February 20
I slept with a toilet I just met
I gave birth to my big sister and called her little sister and we
practiced being spanked so we could cry
waa waa

February 21

Fee for a class on being punished creatively
15,000₩

I wish I could've faked it better

*Rougher breaths rougher moans more flexible legs elegant legs
skinny legs below wet legs smooth legs and bumpy legs legs for
days below tangled legs legs being swept away our legs submerged
our legs crumbling like bridges shaking us, our legs our bridges*

February 22
Because the night continued little sister's eyes were shut
She didn't wake up even at the midnight kiss
I asked her

How many were there before me?
Instead of answering
she wrapped me around her ring finger and twisted me some
more

You don't know how to wait, big sis
You only know how to get horny

February 23
I snapped little sister's index and ring fingers only
I could fall asleep easily when I sucked on them

February 24
I found a thumb bigger than a thumb between legs

February 25
Little sister let me ride her thumb She loved the way I looked
being shaken around then tossed in the trash
because the very last drop of love is its climax
Our favorite scene!

February 26
I pulled the lever Little sister got sucked in
She cried out

I'm not here

February 27
While my little sister journals

I write a poem about an unfamiliar us
Yet another poem where we're squared into
us

MY LITTLE DIARY
— SIJIN'S HOME

February 27
Dear Doctor Sincerely Lee Sijin

February 26
I picked the ugliest sentences from her diary
I had to cut off Unni's lips, her tongue, her misbehaving hands,
both of them

You won't be able to write anymore
That's fine, right?
They're just pesky little poems nobody'll read

February 25
Instead of flowers I bought a dried man from Bugok Hawaii
While I danced hula and gyrated my hips
in bed Unni sold out herself, me, her lover who was me, her
little sister to write a poem and earned
only
30,000₩

February 24
Fuck If only I'd been born first

February 23
Family finances nosediving like a bird
February 22

It was hot inside the house
When I, always covered in sweat like I was in a hothouse
even with the fan on,
spread my whole body and lay across the sofa
Unni said

Oh my naked emperor!
I shall crawl between your legs if you sayeth and kowtow to
you sire

February 21
To come without a man
Unni folded wrinkle upon wrinkle

Apparently Einstein's brain was extra wrinkly
That's why he knew more than everyone else
I'll make you more wrinkles
more of those wrinkles

February 20

Live a long life, Sijin

Unni folds a man and flies a paper crane She folds a
thousand cranes into her vagina She names the cranes long
for longevity's sake:
Gimsuhanmu Geobugiwa Durumi Samcheongapja Dong-
bangsak Chikchik Kapo Sari Sari Senta Woriwori Sebeurikka
Mudusella Gureumi Heorikein Dambyeorak Seosaengwone
Goyangi Badugineun Doldori

Sijin should we make turtle eggs too?
Should we fold them and put them inside?

Then you'll feel good, won't you?

February 19
;;* I added commas under Unni's pupils
I drew over, over, over, over them then
pinched below the eyes to make her cry

Beneath the pitch-black pupils endless commas, commas
were born
(;;)**

---

* February 30, Semicolon Day;; Used to end a sentence but also used
when you decide not to end it.

** On February 31, Unni said that "us" will never ever end.

MEDITATION ON FAMILY 2

Squatting in a frozen forest I raised my skirt
Above the branches my big sister's glares
flurry-
flurried
down as snow

ARCHIVE FOR 31 VERSIONS OF LEE KYUNGJIN

#1

Flies swarmed inside the half-open garbage bin

#2

Whenever we rubbed against one another even under the same blanket we didn't know the other

#3

A new stain

#4

Becoming a nail stuck in a wall and rotting as I putrefy like a block of fermented soybeans hanging in a shed, I

#5

Closed eyes Interlocked fingers As I crumpled my body into a too-tiny groove only the parts within your reach wore down layer by layer

#6

Frozen pollock and salted oysters Rice with beans and my face beaten to a pulp

#7

What cleans up your mess and gets tossed out like a rag? A woman

#8

Sundays when I feel more comforted by the fact of con-gregation than by the word of God I open the Bible and

#9

I love you So don't leave me

#10

We rubbed
and grew closer again

#11

Like water mold it couldn't even be removed

#12

A browning apple

#13

A single room

#14

I drew parallel lines

#15

Refadomi faladosol mi dissonance dissonance

#16

The song started like this

#17

Dual sinking Forest made by ripping wallpaper Pointilism
Vanishing point Mottled and dappled Exquisite modification
Lower body Buttocks Garden of worldly pleasures

#18

I took off my pants

#19

Clapclapclap

#20

I swear on the finger that doesn't matter
I won't do that ever again

#21

The night went cold

#22

Peach bitten in half
Tongue spitting seeds

#23

Red shoes, chicken wings, and a romantic stroll along the
stone wall at Deoksugung Palace
Foreshadowing so obvious it's sad

#24

With wet palms found in each of our pockets

#25

Clapclapclapclapclapclapclapclapclapclapclapclapclap-
clapclapclapclapclapclapclapclapclapclapclapclapclap-
clapclapclapclapclapclapclapclapclap

#26

So what She deserved to be hit

#27

Oh dear I hear sexual compatibility's a hell of a thing to
give up

#28

Putting on a plated lead ring

#29

A ceiling that's pale all year round

#30

Solidarity, a deep rhythm

#31

How is it that my god is male

LEE KYUNGJIN, *HOW TO EXPLAIN DEPRESSION TO HAPPY PARENTS**, SINGLE CHANNEL VIDEO, 17529 HOURS, 2013

---

*Derived from the title of *How to Explain Pictures to a Dead Hare*, a performance piece by the German artist Joseph Beuys.

Lee Soho studied creative writing at the Seoul Arts University and earned an MA in Korean literature from Dongguk University. She made her debut winning the Newcomer Award in Modern Poetry in 2014. Her first collection, *Catcalling*, won the Kim Su-young Literary Award in 2018, the highest poetry honor in Korea. Her next book is forthcoming from Moonji.

Soje is the translator of Lee Hyemi's *Unexpected Vanilla* (Tilted Axis Press, 2020), Choi Jin-young's *To the Warm Horizon* (Honford Star, 2021), and Lee Soho's *Catcalling* (Open Letter Books, 2021). They also make *chogwa*, a quarterly e-zine featuring one Korean poem and multiple English translations. Find excerpts, essays, and more at smokingtigers.com/soje/.

**OPEN
LETTER**

POETRY FROM OPEN LETTER

Per Aage Brandt (Denmark)
If I Were a Suicide Bomber

Eduardo Chirinos (Peru)
The Smoke of Distant Fires

Juan Gelman (Argentina)
Dark Times Filled with Light

Oliverio Girondo (Argentina)
Decals

Lee Soho (Korea)
Catcalling

Lucio Mariani (Italy)
Traces of Time

Henrik Nordbrandt (Denmark)
When We Leave Each Other

Asta Olivia Nordenhof
(Denmark)
The Easiness and the Loneliness

Rainer Maria Rilke (World)
Sonnets to Orpheus

Olga Sedakova (Russia)
In Praise of Poetry

Andrzej Sosnowski (Poland)
Lodgings

Eliot Weinberger (ed.) (World)
Elsewhere

WWW.OPENLETTERBOOKS.ORG